HONDA

M000286357

HONDA

MICK WALKER

OSPREY
AUTOMOTIVE

Published in 1993 by Osprey Publishing Ltd
59 Grosvenor Street, London W1X 9DA

© Osprey 1993

All rights reserved. Apart from any fair
dealing for the purpose of private study,
research, criticism or review, as permitted
under the Copyright, Designs and Patents
Act, no part of this publication may be
reproduced, stored in a retrieval system, or
transmitted in any form or by any means,
electronic, electrical, chemical, mechanical,
optical, photocopying, recording or otherwise,
without prior written permission. All enquiries
should be addressed to the Publishers.

ISBN 1 85532 276 5

All photographs by Don Morley or from Mick
Walker's collection.

Project Editor Shaun Barrington
Copy Editor Aimee Blythe
Page design Paul Kime
Printed in Hong Kong

Half title page
*Freddie Spencer aboard a CB900
during the 1980 Superbike race at
Daytona*

Title page
*Reborn big single; a 1987 XBR500
out in the English countryside*

Right
*The VF500F2 was to prove a superb,
if complex, middleweight sportster
with performance to match the
Kawasaki GPZ600, allied to
beautifully balanced handling and
ultra-safe braking*

Front cover
*John Macdonald putting his CBR600
to good use during 1991's Supercup
races at Snetterton*

Back cover
*Flying high at Daytona USA's
Supercross, 125 cc Pro-link Moto-X
model and rider*

For a catalogue of all books published by Osprey Automotive
please write to:

The Marketing Department, Octopus Illustrated Books,
1st Floor, Michelin House, 81 Fulham Road, London SW3 6RB

Contents

Introduction

At the end of the Second World War, Japan was a shattered country, most of its production facilities and cities little more than masses of rubble. No one could have foreseen the rebirth which was to follow from this scene of utter devastation and, in its wake, the creation of the biggest economic miracle in modern history.

Many of the first generation Japanese post-war motorcycles were crude in the extreme and perhaps none more so than the type built by Soichiro Honda using a batch of war-surplus petrol engines which had formerly been used by the military authorities to power small generators. But these exceedingly basic machines sold like hot cakes in an environment hungry for any form of personal transport. And so the first hesitant steps were taken towards Honda's ultimate emergence as the world's largest motorcycle manufacturer.

A series of events — including near bankruptcy in 1953 — was to see Honda come out at the top of a myriad of small manufacturers which had sprung up in Japan during the late 1940s and early 1950s. By the year 1960, Japan was manufacturing an amazing 1.4 million powered two-wheelers of which a large percentage were of Honda origin. This was in no small part due to the unparalleled success of the 50 cc C100 Super Cub which had been introduced in October 1958; in its first full production year, 1959, an incredible 755,000 Super Cubs were sold.

In 1960 the Japanese led by Honda, began their export drive. This was greatly assisted by three main factors; import restrictions on the home market; an enthusiasm for investment in the future rather than in making quick profits — best illustrated by the high level of research and development and the willingness to sanction an expensive Grand Prix racing budget in a quest for publicity through racing success; and finally the ability to create what the market wanted.

As long ago as February 1954 Soichiro Honda had despatched a works-prepared 125 cc racing machine to take part in the prestigious international Brazilian São Paolo meeting. The machine's subsequent poor showing did nothing to dampen Mr. Honda's will to succeed, and later that year during a European visit — in which he visited the Isle of Man TT — he took a special interest in the highly organised, all-conquering German NSU team, modelling his efforts thereafter in a similar fashion.

Honda did not return to the Isle of Man for another five years, when in 1959, a team of twin cylinder 125 cc machines, led by chief engineer Niisuma and American advisor Bill Hunt (who doubled as a rider), gained considerable publicity by winning the team prize. This was only the start, Yamaha and Suzuki joined Honda when they returned to the TT in 1960, and although there wasn't a Japanese victory, the writing was clearly on the wall for all those who wanted to see.

The Japanese quickly realised that besides technical wizardry they also needed top line riders — and this meant signing established western stars. For example Honda's 1961 squad consisted of not only four Japanese, but also Jim Redman, Tom Phillis, Mike Hailwood and Bob McIntyre. The net result was the first Japanese world championship trophies and TT victories; Phillis and Redman became 125 and 250 cc champions respectively, whilst Hailwood chalked up an impressive TT double.

This was the spring board from which Honda quickly followed by Suzuki and Yamaha, and finally Kawasaki simply steamrollered the opposition. There followed a frantic battle between the Japanese 'big four' for racing honours which saw the most amazing array of design; from Honda's jewel-like 50 cc dohc twin which revved to over 22,000 rpm, to models with up to five or six cylinders for the 125 and 250 cc class respectively. Only in the 500 cc and sidecar categories did non-Japanese machines continue to prosper. Later this sporting expertise was extended to other fields including motocross, trials and enduro.

Meanwhile the European manufacturers, already outgunned in sporting events, soon found themselves overhauled in the standard production sector. This was most obvious in the lucrative American market, where the Japanese sold a host of multi cylinder models at highly competitive prices which appealed to the Stateside consumer. The Japanese motorcycle boom of the 1960s attracted many a newcomer to two-wheels; Honda again leading the way, typified by their advertising slogan; 'You meet the nicest people on a Honda'.

Only in the bigger classes did the Europeans and American (the latter in effect now meaning a single marque, Harley Davidson) continue to offer a credible challenge. But even this was severely dented when the

first of the new four cylinder Honda CB750s appeared in 1968. From then on nothing could stem the Japanese sales effort, which not only owed its phenomenal success to the high quality of its products, but also to an unsurpassed marketing machine. Other manufacturers, including rivals Suzuki, Yamaha and Kawasaki, could only look on in envy as Honda pumped out millions of motorcycles, which sold all around the world.

Honda's NX650 Dominator uses 4-valve technology first developed on the XL250 of the early 1970s.

Soichiro Honda died in August 1991, but not before having the great satisfaction of seeing the company which bears his name firmly established as the largest and most powerful motorcycle manufacturer in history.

Early Days

As recounted in the Introduction Soichiro Honda had survived a number of problems including near bankruptcy, to see his company become the largest and most successful motorcycle manufacturer in Japan by the end of the 1950s. Much of this early success had been due to the high sales gained by one model, the 50 cc Super Cub.

As the 1960s dawned Honda was therefore in a strong position to meet its creator's big dream – the export markets of the world.

The first Honda twin cylinder roadster had been developed by the company's research team back in 1957. This featured an all-aluminium engine with a capacity of 247 cc and single overhead camshaft. Unusually, both frame, swinging arm and the front leading forks were manufactured from pressed steel sheet. The C70 Dream, as it was called, proved a revelation with its high level of sophistication which included state-of-the-art lighting, electrics and switchgear. The following year the design was equipped with an electric starter, and in February 1959 the C72 Dream was displayed at the Amsterdam Show – the first ever Japanese motorcycle to appear at a major European event. With its class leading 20 bhp on tap, a claimed 85 mph and a luxury specification the new Honda completely overshadowed its various European competitors.

Right
Honda's first machine was powered by a war surplus 50 cc two-stroke engine conceived to power military generators. Nicknamed the 'chimney', 500 were constructed in the immediate post-war days

Opposite
The 1949 90 cc B-type. This was the company's first real production model and once again the engine was a single cylinder two-stroke

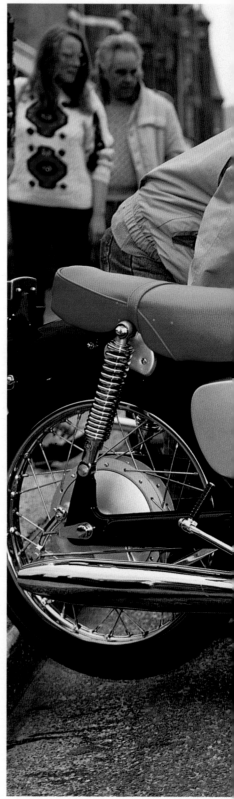

Above
Much of Honda's early success was due to one model, the C100 Super Cub, which was introduced in 1958. During its first full production year an incredible 755,000 examples were sold

Right
The CB92 was a popular choice with sporting riders of the early 1960s; today it's viewed as a classic of its kind

This was to prove the launch pad for the Japanese company's incredible explosion onto the world stage. That same year not only saw the first Honda compete in the Isle of Man TT, but an American subsidiary set up in California.

From a mere 96 bikes in that first year, the USA saw over 65,000 Hondas sold by 1962, some 50 per cent of the total market.

The first exports to Europe had come in 1957 (albeit in very small numbers) and by 1960 considerable numbers of C100 Super Cub, C92 and C72 were being shipped. Soon afterwards sporting models such as the CB92, CB72 and CB160 became available both in Europe and the USA.

In 1961, as a flood of new Cubs, Benlys and Dreams flowed off their production lines back home, Honda established their very first overseas manufacturing facility in Taiwan, off the mainland of China.

Above
A race-kitted CB92 at Snetterton circuit, summer 1964

Left
The fastest and most powerful production Japanese bike of its era was the 1964 305 cc CB77 (Hawk in USA)

Two years later, in 1963, a subsidiary was established in Belgium to assemble and market mopeds throughout the Common Market. That same year a larger version of the Dream, the C77 appeared with an engine capacity of 305cc, together with a new 90cc model.

One notable failure amongst a horde of success stories was the Juno scooter, which although available over several years failed to catch the public's attention.

The fastest and most powerful production Japanese bike of its era was the 1964 28.5 bhp 305cc CB77 Super Sports (Hawk in the USA) twin. British road tests of the time revealed that with its 95 mph top speed it was more than a match for several of the 500cc twins from

Above
The Honda stand at the London Earls Court Show, autumn 1964

Right
American market CL77. This was basically a 'street scrambler' version of the 305 cc CB77 street bike, with hi-level pipes, braced 'bars and revised styling

such notable companies as BSA, Norton and Triumph. The story of Honda right from the beginning has been one of continuous expansion, fuelled by constant development and model changes. The following chapters outline the inexorable progress, highlighting the watershed production machines and the international sporting successes of this awesome motorcycle marque.

Black Bomber

First news of an impending Japanese onslaught on that bastion of the British motorcycle industry, the big four-stroke twin, came in 1964, when a visiting journalist discovered an entirely new 500-class vertical twin. This machine, styled on British lines, was seen undergoing 'secret' tests on Honda's test track.

At the time everyone – at least outside Japan – believed that the Japanese had left the production of larger capacity machines to other nations, such as Britain, and would limit their efforts to a total concentration of the lightweight market.

The new machine, later to be identified as the Honda CB450 Black Bomber (thanks to the machines advertising campaign), was the very motorcycle the British industry had thought, hoped and prayed the Japanese would never make. And as subsequent events were to prove, it was this machine which heralded the final era of what was – in retrospect – the final push for supremacy from the industrial warriors of Nippon, culminating a few short years later with the really big guns headed by Honda's CB750 four.

For firms such as BSA, Triumph and AMC, the 305 cc CB77 had signalled the limit of how far the Japanese had intended advancing. The CB77 was only an overbored CB72 250, although fast at a genuine 95 mph, and no match in the grunt department for the 650 cc British twins.

Honda, having successfully attacked the lightweight sector, had set their sights higher and needing a flagship saw the CB450 as just such a machine. Something which could perform against the opposition on both motorways and back roads, the dreaded Black Bomber or Dragon, as it was sometimes called, was just that – at least on paper.

The first of the new breed appeared on British roads in 1965, when Honda UK's first CB450 test bike arrived and was eagerly sought out by British journalists.

FYN 444C soon proved that it was a sports tourer – rather than an out-and-out sportster – as many a scribe had predicted. Having said that, it proved to have a genuine 100 mph potential coupled with a modern engine design, outstanding brakes and a high standard of reliability. The only fly in the ointment was in the handling department, where there was still plenty of room for improvement.

For most engineers in the 1960s, tradition was something to be followed – but not at Honda. Their earlier designs had shown that they were far too enterprising to follow tradition. With the engine of their CB450 this love of technical innovation had been taken a stage

CB450 Black (this one's red!) Bomber caused havoc amongst the senior management of the British bike industry when it was launched in 1965

Hi-tech 445 cc (70 ×57.8mm) engine featured dohc, torsion bar valve springs and a mind blowing 8500 rpm

further, in the shape of several features which departed from the engineering norm.

Most obvious for a roadster of the period, were its twin overhead camshafts. Next came their method of drive, namely by a long chain from a 16-tooth sprocket in the middle of the crankshaft. Then there were torsion bar valve springs, a 180° crankshaft and − for the time − a mind-blowing peak rpm of 8500.

The most novel of these features was the use of torsion bar valve springs. What were they? Well, torsion means twist. Each torsion bar was a short, stiff length of spring steel, splined at both ends. One end was anchored in a retainer bolted to the cylinder head; the other end was splined into a tubular guide which itself was splined into the pivot end of a forked arm, which in turn closed the valve.

During engine assembly the bar was given a slight twist by a tool engaged with the retainer, before this was clamped to the head. This ensured that the forked arm exerted a firm pressure on the valve collar. When the valve was opened by the cam follower the arm was pivoted downwards, turning the guide with it, and in doing so imparting a further twist to the bar. As the cam relaxed its pressure the wire untwisted, turning the guide and arm back again to close the valve.

In reality there was nothing really unusual in twisting a length of rod to get a spring effect. This is the very principle of the ordinary coil valve spring − which is simply a long, thin torsion bar coiled up for compact installation.

What Honda engineers displayed with the CB450 engine design was a principle used successfully by the Japanese even today; unveiling previously used technical features with effective marketing or in the guise of totally new innovation. And in their most noteworthy designs, such as the CB450, it was usually a combination of the two.

Honda claimed the engine developed 43 bhp (at the crankshaft) and 98 mph. Out on the road an early Motor Cycle road test managed a 101 mph speed from the 445 cc (70 × 57.8mm) short stroke unit with the tester commenting: 'Without question the CB450 is the most impressive Honda to leave Japan'. The quietness of the engine was also noted. This was due in part to the valve clearances, which were minimal.

Early engines used a single points set up, but this was soon discarded in favour of twin contact breakers, one pair just not being able to provide enough sparks for the 12-volt ignition.

There were a total of four caged roller main bearings, with caged roller big ends, and the 8.5:1 compression pistons featured three rings. Primary drive was by spur gears, secondary by chain.

For the 1968 model year Honda's middleweight twin became the CB450K1; besides revised styling, the gearbox was given an additional ratio, making five in all

The cycle parts closely followed those of the CB72/77 series, and although much of this was good, the tyres and suspension are best described as abysmal. The rear suspension and to a lesser extent the front forks — providing a pogo-stick effect, which combined with tyres almost totally lacking in grip didn't exactly inspire confidence!

Motor Cycle, in a special 'Honda Supplement' published during 1966, went as far as a comment about instability in the wet.

With a tank full of petrol, the CB450 tipped the scales at almost 204 kg, some 34 kg higher than the Triumph T100SS — its nearest British competitor. So although offering a list of technical features it was also considerably heavier, heavier in fact than a 650 Bonneville!

But the biggest difference between the Japanese newcomer and the traditional British big twin was engine torque. To extract its full performance potential the Honda had to be revved. Up to 6000 rpm the performance was nothing special, but from that figure the CB450 showed its real colours, with all previous vibration disappearing as the bike screamed forward towards the horizon.

All those high revolutions caused the pundits to opinion that the CB450's engine wouldn't last long. But providing the oil was religiously changed at 1000 mile intervals, it was remarkably free of major hassles. Another don't, involved not revving the engine hard while still cold. This was because the oilways were very small, but the main engine power was developed at the top end of the scale. The owner's handbook actually stated quite clearly (almost a Government Health-type warning!): 'Leave the bike ticking over for about 2 minutes before riding off'.

In fact tickover problems (even with the choke off) were a source of trouble on early model CB450s, to the extent that Honda even went as far as issuing a special kit to dealers to overcome this.

Then there was the price, at £360 it was more expensive than virtually any British bike — for example it was possible to buy a brand new BSA 650 Lightning from Comerfords for only £308 at the time. Yet initial press reaction was enthusiastic around the world, and nowhere more so than in Britain.

Because of this Honda made a commercial error for the 1966 season, by diverting a complete shipment of American bound CB450s to Britain. These US specification bikes had small turn signals and a different wiring loom, which does not match any of the diagrams in the official Honda Workshop Manual.

Unfortunately for the company, 1966 witnessed a sudden fall in British motorcycle sales (hence the cheap BSA Lightnings) leaving Honda with a relatively large number of unsold machines — a not uncommon experience throughout the industry.

These took some time to be cleared, and resulted in Ken Ives of Leicester, then one of the major Honda UK dealers, purchasing a large number of CB450s at a heavily discounted price. But instead of marketing them simply as discounted machines to the public, he offered them in cafe racer form at some £15 below list price. The specification included clip-ons, chrome plated mudguards and headlamp, fork gaiters – the customer could even specify his own choice of colour for the tank and sidepanels. This stylish package sold like hot cakes, turning what had been a poor seller into a dream machine which attracted many youngsters moving up from their smaller CB92 and CB72s.

Another controversy which surrounded the CB450's British appearance centred around Hondas corporate marketing campaign. A whole string of adverts appeared depicting a CB450 compared with certain British bikes – including an ancient 1952 BSA plunger framed twin and, worse still, to many a British bike buff a Vincent V-twin. Comparing the cheeky Japanese invader to a BSA was bad enough but a Vincent – this was just sacrilege! Phone lines were soon buzzing at Hondas Power Road headquarters.

In the USA, the CB450 (and later 500T) gained more respect than in any other world market. The popular 450CL variant was introduced in 1967 and reflected the street scrambling craze of that time sweeping the North American continent. The CL had a higher 9:1 compression ratio, even though maximum torque was kicked out lower down the scale. Combined with lower gearing, this meant a far more flexible engine response.

Late in 1967, a new version appeared which had a revised chassis with the wheelbase extended from 53 inches to 54 inches. There were changes to the engine assembly as well, the most striking of these being the gearbox, which was now a five speeder. Maximum power had also risen to 45 bhp at 9000 rpm. The fuel tank was reshaped as were the sidepanels, while the instruments now sat separately above the top yoke.

The first British riders saw of the new model was at the Earls Court Show in September that year. Gone was the Black Bomber image, for the five-speed CB450 had a bright red finish, and a price tag of £365. 1968 was also the year that the parent company produced their ten millionth bike, and Soichiro Honda himself rode the garlanded machine off the production line in a blaze of publicity.

It was fitting that this machine was a CB450, the first of an unstoppable tide of larger capacity bikes from Japan that were to finally extinguish the guttering flame of the British motorcycle industry.

1968 was also the year that the company produced its ten millionth bike, and Soichiro Honda is seen here riding the garlanded machine (a CB450K1) off the production line in a blaze of glory

CB750 – the original Superbike

.What is meant by the term 'big bike'? Well, in British terms anything above 650 seemed big until the 1960s when the Triumph and BSA triples were felt to be large machines. It has become commonplace today to think of some machines as being 'only' 500 cc when all the Japanese manufacturers produce bikes of over 1,000 cc. These are the so-called superbikes, a term which hadn't been coined in the sixties when the Honda CB750 first made its appearance. This was the first of the breed, and nowadays the CB750 is widely believed to be the first superbike.

For the serious motorcyclist in the mid-sixties, the parallel twin was the obvious choice, probably a Triumph or a Norton with a displacement of around 650 cc, and it was widely rumoured that Honda would go the same way and introduce a 750 cc parallel twin machine. No one believed that the kind of engineering complexity seen in the four cylinder racer would be embodied in a road-going motorcycle. When the machine turned out to be a four-cylinder model derived very noticeably from the racer, only with a single cam, it had a profound impact.

The CB750 was first introduced to the public at the Tokyo Show in October 1968 and launched in America, where Honda had been selling bikes for ten years, in the January of 1969. The price was set at just a little more than the Rocket Three or the Trident and was seen to be very competitive for such a daring and innovative machine. Although there was an enthusiastic response to the new bike in Europe, most of the early production went to America.

From then on the days of the large capacity parallel twin were numbered, even though the only other fours one could buy were rather exclusive and exotic, such as the MV Agusta.

With the great conservatism in the world's motorcycle industry, Honda took a brave step indeed with the CB750, and it turned out to be the bike which really launched them as a world market leader. The machine was radical and different; ironic when the four-cylinder Japanese bike has today become somewhat irreverently known as the 'UJM', the Universal Japanese Motorcycle, with all the Big Four manufacturers using this configuration. In its historical context, the CB750 was little short of fantastic; it was civilised, it started at the touch of a button and yet it had, for then, electrifying performance.

The CB750 created an impression of superb style and engineering

The first CB750 – the motorcycle which coined the word Superbike. Launched at the Tokyo Show in October 1968, it went on sale shortly afterwards

but it was not, of course, faultless. The engine required careful and regular servicing if it was to remain sweet-running, with some owners of high-mileage examples swearing that oil changes every thousand miles were the answer to longevity. The engine was a free-revving and sweet unit with few obvious vices. The chassis of the early machine, however, came in for much criticism for its general sloppiness. But to be fair the original tyres were not very good, and the rear suspension units were too soggy; some attention here could pay great dividends.

Although the later 750s were dohc the early ones had a single overhead camshaft driven by an endless chain. The camshaft ran in the centre of the cylinder head and was supported by four plain bearing surfaces and was retained by end-caps, the drive-chain running in a central tunnel between the middle two cylinders. There were two valves per cylinder, with the valves being actuated by short, stiff arms pivoting on shafts lying parallel to the camshaft.

With five plain bearings to support it, the crankshaft was of one-piece construction with the alternator mounted on the left hand end. In the centre was the sprocket for the camshaft drive-chain and the duplex primary drive sprocket, both of integral construction with the crank. Cam-drive chains were to prove troublesome and noisy in operation. The contact breaker was driven from the right hand end of the crankshaft.

The wet multiplate clutch was driven from the right hand end of the gearbox imput shaft and there were five speeds with a drum-type selector shaft and forks. Overall ratios were 14.01, 9.57, 7.45, 6.25 and 5.26 to 1. In its original form the engine was dry-sump lubricated, with a frame mounted oil tank, the system having a capacity of six pints. The oil was pressurised by a single trochoid-type pump driven from the kickstart pinion, with the oil being filtered by a renewable element mounted at the front of the engine. The whole engine unit was of light alloy construction and the cylinder barrels were heavily finned, with the alternator and points covers being highly polished.

The frame was of duplex construction of welded tubular steel. The front telescopic fork was oil damped, while a pivoted fork and twin spring-damper units took care of the rear suspension. Braking was courtesy of a single front disc and a rear drum brake. The electrical system was 12-volt, powered by a three-phase alternator and the machine had electric starting as standard. A striking feature of the early 750 was the four into four exhaust system, unfortunately this was extremely expensive to replace.

A wide range of aftermarket accessories became available for the machine such as four-into-one exhaust systems and big-bore kits,

CB750 was powered by a single overhead cam 736.5 cc (61 ×63mm) engine. Maximum power output was 67 bhp at 8000 rpm, giving a top speed of around 115 mph

Above
The 750 four remained virtually unchanged for a number of years: this is an early 1970s model finished in metallic bronze

Right
Honda's first 750 four cylinder racer was based around the CB750. The bike shown here is the actual machine on which Dick Mann won the 1970 Daytona 200

notably from Action Four and Yoshimura. The handling could be improved by the fitment of taper-roller steering-head bearing conversions, British tyres such as Avon Roadrunners or Dunlop TT 100's and Girling gas-filled shock absorbers.

The engine was steadily developed until 1978 when the dohc version replaced the original single camshaft model, by which time Kawasaki and Suzuki's were proving to be serious competitors. However, Honda had already begun to respond to the growing challenge by introducing, in 1975, the CB750 F1 with much revised steering geometry and other chassis changes to try to cure the poor handling.

Road-tests of the original model waxed lyrical about the virtues of such a radically different motorcycle, with tales of effortless smoothness and the seemingly endless flow of power, despite the

Above
First real update for the CB750
came with the 750F in 1975. This
employed 'Euro' styling similar to
that used on the smaller CB400F

Right
World Champion Phil Read riding
the new 750F2 in 1977

tingling of vibration through the footrests and bars. For a road-going machine to still be accelerating above the magic ton was something seldom experienced. At the time it was the fastest bike over the standing quarter ever tested by some journals. Top speed was in the region of 118 mph with the standing quarter coming up in around 14 seconds and 100 mph. A gallon of petrol was consumed at between 40-50 mile intervals, depending on how hard the machine was ridden.

The original CB750, of which few survive today, was a truly great and innovative motorcycle. A trendsetter which spawned a whole generation of superbikes, which are only now beginning to be replaced by the so-called new engine configurations.

Above
Four pipe CB750K featured dohc engine first used in 1979

Right
To cash in on the 'Retro' craze Honda recreated the CB750 (Nighthawk in the USA) in 1991. This 'back-to-basics' street bike, epitomizes the almost timeless qualities that made Honda famous in the big-bike league

Right

The Swiss star, Luigi Taveri rode for the Honda works team from 1962 to 1966. He was world champion in the 125 cc category in 1961, 1964 and again in 1966. Taveri is shown here on a 250 four in the Italian GP at Monza, the machine which won the world championship in 1961, 1962 and 1963

Above

Not content with winning world titles, Honda also produced a series of successful 'over-the-counter' racers. These included the 50 cc CR110 single...

Jim Redman had joined the team at the Dutch TT, whilst, sadly, Bob Brown suffered a fatal accident at the German round.

Then it was back to Japan and a winter of feverish development on the machinery, whilst more signings were made with top British riders Bob McIntyre and the brilliant young Mike Hailwood joining the Japanese squad.

With a new European racing headquarters in Hanover, the team now comprised eight riders. With much improved bikes (the 1961 twin, gave 20 bhp, the four over 40 bhp) and a formidable array of stars success looked to be assured. As so it was; with Phillis and Hailwood becoming the new 125 and 250 cc world road racing champions, Hondas only real threat that year being the East German MZ two-strokes in the smaller category.

...and 125 cc CR93 twin, one of which is seen here with British Champion, Rod Scivyer aboard in the mid 1960s

Above
*Close-up of Honda's jewel-like 50 cc dohc twin which revved to over 22,000 rpm.
Ridden by Irishman Ralph Bryans, it took Honda's only world title in the
tiddler class, circa 1965*

Right
*The amazing five cylinder 125 made its debut at the Japanese GP in October
1965, finishing a close second to Ernst Degner's Suzuki; it went on to take the
championship in the following year*

1962 saw four classes instead of two contested, with new bikes
for the 50 cc and 350 cc categories. Again Honda didn't take the
championship first time out, but it learned what was needed in the 350
cc, although it took longer to build a race winner in the tiddler class.
Finally, for the 1966 season Honda re-signed Mike Hailwood (he had
ridden for MV Agusta from 1962–1965) to race in the blue riband 500
cc class with an enlarged version of their classic four cylinder design.
But even Hailwoods mastery couldn't bring Soichiro Honda's company
the ultimate prize. But by the time the Japanese concern quit the GP
scene at the end of 1967 it could boast a superb 16 world titles –
50 cc (1), 125 cc (4), 250 cc (5) and 350 cc (6). These had been gained
by a range of multi-cylinder four-strokes with two, four, five or six

Above
Giving his all – multi world champion Carl Fogarty contesting 1989's World Superbike Championships on a privcately entered Honda RC30 at Donington Park

Left
A legend from an earlier era. After leaving Honda to race Italian MV's, Mike Hailwood returned to the Japanese marque for the 1966 season. He beat former team mate Giacomo Agostini to become the new 350 world champion on this 297 cc six cylinder model

Above
Honda attempted a return to Grand Prix racing in 1979 with the ultra-complex NR500. This pioneered the use of the now-famous 'oval' bores, twin-choke carburettors and double con-rods to prevent the pistons from tilting. Track results didn't live up to the promise of the technical gizmos

Left
After Honda retired from Grand Prix racing at the end of 1967, its next big venture on the tarmac came during the mid 1970s in the world of endurance racing. Here the winners of the 1977 Le Mans 24 hour race, Léon and Chemarin, look on as mechanics work on their 997 cc four cylinder model

cylinders. And in the process Honda had helped make the 1960s one of the truly great decades in the history of motorcycle racing.

What came afterwards was always something of an anti-climax – even wins in the Daytona 200, the World Endurance championship, Barcelona 24 hours plus more TT and Grand Prix victories; none would quite match up to the incredible technical advancement made during those golden days of the 1960s.

Above
Takazumi Katayama giving the NR500 one of its few outings at the Belgian GP in July 1979

Right
All the excitement of the classic Daytona 200 is captured in this 1984 shot showing Honda stars Merkel and Spencer amongst a pack of riders approaching the first turn

Overleaf
Following in the footsteps of Spencer and later Wayne Gardner, Australian Mick Doohan emerged as Honda's leading rider in the all-important blue riband 500 cc class at the beginning of the 1990s

Above
1991 and 1992 World 250 cc Champion Luca Cadalora of Italy seen here clinching the 1992 title on his NSR 250 Honda at the British Grand Prix at Donington

Right
Besides its GP successes, Honda has continued its love affair with the Isle of Man TT series. In 1991 the company scored a 1-2-3 in the Senior event. Steve Hislop (centre) won from Phil McCallen and Joey Dunlop

CD Series

The machines that are the Cinderellas of the motorcycling world are those that don't have startling performance, but are reliable above all else. You can't boast about their performance so they don't appear in motorcycle magazine tests, and are not pushed by the manufacturers in adverts, especially since the early 1970s when the superbike was introduced.

One such machine is the Honda CD175. The bike was sold in various forms for over ten years and then updated to a 185. It had a final upgrade to 200 cc before it was killed off only to be reborn as the CB 250 during the late 1980s.

Introduced to the UK market in April 1967 for the grand sum of 159 guineas (the way all high-class auctioneers and dubious secondhand car dealers priced the goods for sale at the time), it was a sales success from the start. The CD175 came as standard with large direction indicators, prop-stand, fully enclosed chain, steering lock, ignition lock and had colour-matched valanced plastic mudguards, headlamp shell and toolbox cover. The CD175A as sold in Britain did not have an electric start as did the CD175A sold elsewhere.

The frame followed Honda design of the time. T-shaped pressed steel with the swinging arm also being pressed steel. Telescopic forms and fully enclosed rear shocks provided the suspension.

Buyers were sometimes put off by the fact that the frame was unfinished inside. This did not seem to be a problem as long as the bike was kept undercover most of the time, and in general frames seem to have lasted well.

The twin-cylinder engine was from the family of engines that powered the CB125 and CB160. It now had a 180° crank carried on three roller and one ball main bearings. The single overhead cam was driven from the centre of the crank via a roller chain and ran directly in the alloy head. The engine had a single Keihin PW-22 carb with lever operated choke and a paper element air filter. The alloy barrels were inclined 30° forward which is the hallmark of this model. A 52 × 41mm bore and stroke and a compression ratio of 9:1 gave a maximum torque at a high 8000 rpm, with max revs of 10,000. The battery was a six-volt unit producing 10.5 amps per hour and fed a 30/35 W headlight. Ignition was the conventional points and coil setup.

The drive to the four-speed gearbox was by helical gears between the crank and clutch drum, and then through a five-plate clutch to the actual gearbox. Like most Honda clutches it is light and smooth in operation. Wet sump lubrication followed normal Honda practice, with

First version of the CD175 as it appeared in 1967. Notable features included pressed steel frame, fully enclosed rear chain and enclosed suspension, plus steeply inclined cylinders for single overhead cam twin cylinder engine

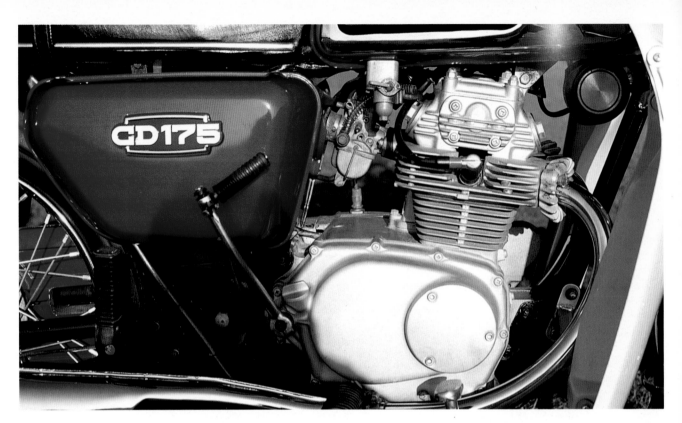

the oil pump driven off an eccentric cam on the back of the clutch. Total oil capacity is 2.7 pints, filtered via a crank driven centrifugal filter. Early owners' handbooks specify a monograde oil for the engine, this can however be substituted by a modern multigrade.

A six-inch single leading shoe front brake and a 5.75 inch SLS rear brake provided the stopping power. Both front and rear wheels are 16 inch.

The bike was quickly recognised as a cheap to run, a reliable 'go to work' machine that doubled up at weekends as a modest tourer, and for many it was the first machine they owned. Performance was reasonable with a claimed top speed of 80 mph and with average use would return 80 mpg.

The CD175 was updated in 1970 with a total redesign of cycle parts, although the basic concept remained the same.

The only real engine change was to reduce the forward lean of the barrels to a mere eight degrees. It still produced 17 bhp and retained the four-speed gearbox and six-volt electrics. Major changes, however, took place to the frame. The CD now had a semi-tubular frame which resulted in a few cosmetic changes. Tank was now more rounded, the plastic mudguards were replaced with steel ones while side covers and headlight shell remained plastic. The more upright barrels necessitated a few changes to the exhaust pipes and the silencers. This new model also came in two new colours, candy red or candy blue.

The next model to be released, the CD175A4, had some minor changes to exhaust specs and carb plus a redesigned air cleaner. A few more minor changes were seen when the CD175A5 came along but it remained pretty much the same. The next redesign came with the introduction of the CD185.

The CD175 and its variants collected an enthusiastic following from owners, especially the earlier models, on which many of today's motorcyclists started their two-wheel life. They were also used and abused by local councils for Park Rangers, Police, Post Office and any courier firms that wanted a simple machine for town work.

A 'Riders Report' in Motor Cycle during 1969 had very little criticism of the machine. Ninety per cent of the riders were happy with it and said they would buy another Honda machine (that was back in the good old pre-soft cams and cam chain problem days). Comments were made on the 'plastic' Japanese tyres which, combined with soft suspension, didn't give the best handling in the world. Lack of damping could be improved dramatically by fitting Girling suspension units and a new set of British tyres. The biggest complaint at the time was about the length of time to get spares and the price when they arrived. Things haven't changed over the years, have they?

Above left
CD175 'Mark 2' engine featured more upright cylinders, giving a mere 8 degrees. It still produced 17 bhp and retained the four-speed gearbox and six-volt electrics of the original

Below left
Honda offered several optional extras for the CD175, including the legshields shown on this example owned by John Barker

The long running CD175 was finally axed in 1977. However, the following year Honda brought out the CD185T − essentially the same commuter concept, but dressed in revised styling and with a totally different engine. Now featuring crankshaft mounted contact breaker instead of camshaft mounted and vertically split crankcases as opposed to horizontal; from a power output point of view these changes were less significant with only 1 bhp being added over the 175 model.

The 185 itself was superseded in the capacity race by the CD200T in 1980, followed by the CD200TB in 1981. There was also a CM200 custom version which catered for the factory custom craze of that era. These later versions whilst acknowledging such modern technology as 12 volt electrics and CD1 ignition, were still basic no frills (or thrills!) commuter bikes − which, at the end of the day, is all these urban dwellers were meant to be.

The CD200 fell victim of the recession which swept the motorcycle industry in the early-mid 1980s, but towards the end of the decade Honda saw fit to re-introduce their four-stroke twin cylinder commuter concept in the shape of the new CD250U. Although the company were keen to keep the concept, they were also keen to point out that the 250 was not just a re-vamped 200, but had to be treated as a completely new model.

Close examination of the 250 does reveal several changes. Most obvious is the transfer from the dated looking fully shrouded front forks to just gaiters, and no shrouds at all over the rear shocks. Of more practical significance is the loss of the fully enclosed chain case.

The 360 degree twin cylinder four-stroke looks basically the same as the CD200 but hides many differences. With square bore and stroke of 53×53mm capacity is now 233 cc. Deep finning on the barrel gives it an almost two-stroke appearance, but still has it's work cut out trying to keep the cylinders cool as the motor seems to run hot very quickly. The engine cases and head are different from the 200, as is the carburation which is now by two 26mm CV carbs, increasing power output over the 200 model to 21 bhp. Exhausting through a 2 into 2 system, the 250 features a balance pipe where the previous CD's did not. The exhaust note is virtually inaudible, and any passer-by is more likely to be deafened by the tappets! The gearbox, however, gained another cog which does make the engine less frantic at speed.

In 1977 the long running CD175 was axed in favour of the CD185. The 185 was superseded in the capacity race by the CM200 in 1980. A custom version, together with a 125 (shown), were also offered

Left
Honda brochures for the CD200T Benley...

Below left
...and its replacement, the current CD250U

Another bread and butter commuter bike, the CB250 RS. Conquer this market, and you conquer the world; something the Japanese manufacturers understood only too well; too well, that is, for British management of the 1970s

The single downtube frame does nothing to improve the handling over previous models, and in this respect it is a typical 1970s machine – great in a straight line but unforgiving in the corners. Suspension up front seems improved and is reasonably taut, only dipping noticeably under heavy braking. Unfortunately the rear suspension is pure 1970s, soggy and underdamped.

Even though the CD250, like its forerunners, is near the bottom when it comes to handling and roadholding abilities it was after all never intended as anything other than a humble commuter – and with its long pedigree as a reliable and undemanding mode of transport it has few, if any, peers.

CB400F – Euro special

Despite its relatively short model life, the tale of the CB400F is a fascinating one; it being the very first of Honda's Eurobikes. This concept came about in the mid 1970s because the sales graphs in North America were levelling off and the Japanese giant made a decision to target the European market in an attempt to boast sales. This 'Euro' styling was very understated with a distinct absence of the brash crop of colourful decals and metallic paint associated with the company's stateside models of the era. The resulting first effort was destined to become not only a best seller in its intended market, but also a classic in the years to come.

In its original guise the CB400F was a restyled and revamped version of Honda's earlier 350 four cylinder model (never sold in Britain). The actual capacity was just over its designated size at 408 cc (51×50mm bore and stroke dimensions). The single overhead camshaft being driven by a simplex chain from the centre of the crankshaft. Valve operation followed conventional Honda practice with rockers running off a central cam, clearance for both inlet and exhaust tappets being maintained by adjusters at the valve end. Four 20mm Keihan carbs supplied the fuel and breathed through a collective filter box. At the other end of the cylinders, a superbly crafted set of four

Right
Launched in 1975, the 'Euro' styled CB400F soon became a best seller, with some 16,200 examples alone, being sold in Britain over a three year period

Opposite
Exhaust pipes sculpted to an exact line so all four came together to run parallel and then back as one; a distinctive feature of Honda's 408.6 cc four cylinder masterpiece

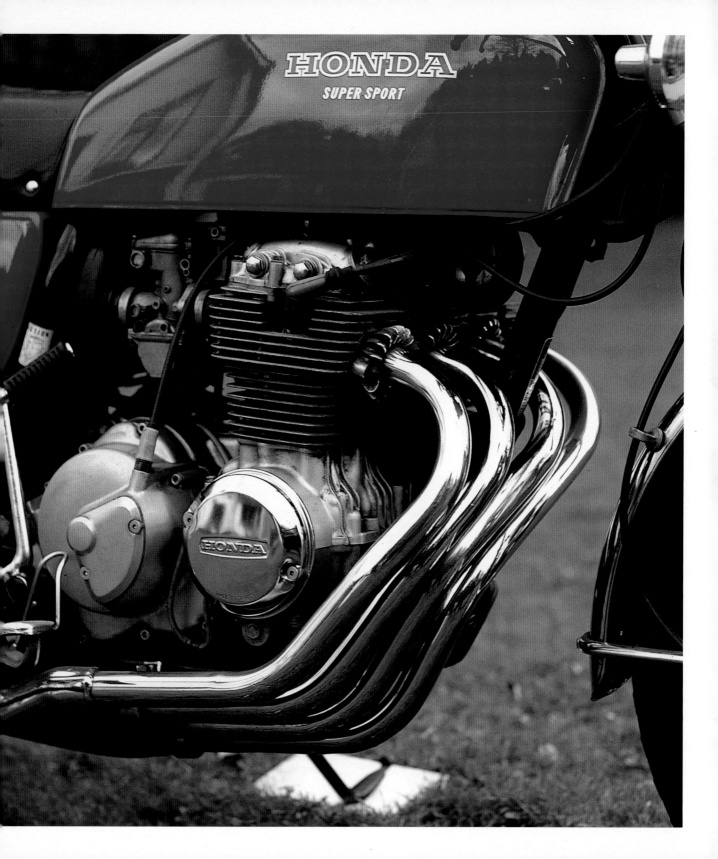

Right
A 1975 photograph showing the earliest (a 1911 Belgian FN) and the latest in four cylinder middleweights

Opposite
For 1976 the model designation changed from F to F2; but except for new cosmetics in the shape of revised colours and decals, plus the addition of pillion footrest hangers, the bike remained as before. Proof if any was needed, of the correctness in the original concept and its design

exhaust pipes ran into a collector box and single silencer on the offside of the machine. The sweep of the pipes was sculpted to an exact line so all four came together to run parallel and then back as one. The exhaust system, together with a six-speed gearbox were two notable features of the machine.

Though it did its job well, the frame was nothing more than the standard of the day with its single spine and front downtube which split to cradle the motor underneath. Likewise the suspension, whilst the 18-inch spoked wheels were shod with a 3.00 section ribbed tyre at the front and a 3.50 blocked pattern at the rear. A single 260mm (10.3 inch) hydraulically operated disc did the stopping up front, backed up by a single leading shoe drum of 170mm (6.7 inch) at the rear.

As far as maintenance is concerned the ignition, clutch adjustment and oil filter are all easy to get at. However, the adjustment area for the contact breaker point can cause problems, as can front disc caliper seizure and rotting mudguards. Even so, the CB400F is one of the all-time classics of Japanese motorcycles; although it has to be said that it never sold in any quantities on the American market. In Britain some 16,200 examples were sold during its three years of imports between 1975 and 1977. During this period there were very little changes apart from colour. For 1976 the model designation changed from F to F2; but except for the cosmetics the addition of pillion footrest hangers

was the only difference. Prior to this the rests were mounted on the swinging arm. The final couple of batches were also supplied with drilled front discs which marginally improved braking response times in wet weather.

So why then did this middleweight four inspire such a strong following? With 37 bhp on tap and a dry weight of 405 kg (184 lbs) maximum speed was a shade over 100 mph it was the first of the modern four cylinder sports roadsters to offer the combination of a turbine smooth power delivery together with nimble, secure handling, and a much superior fuel economy to its largely two-stroke competition.

Many testers of the day saw it as a sports bike with manners. Best summed up by Motor Cycle's John Nutting in the following manner during a 1975 road test: 'It cruises at 45 mph with all the serene grace of a Royal Garden Party. It purrs and coos with all the soft innocence of a pair of doves. But drop down two or three gears and gun it and Honda's new CB400 four transforms into a tyre-spinning, screaming 10,000 rpm re-incarnation of a grand prix bike'.

Looking back, perhaps the bike's biggest claim to fame is that it almost invented the now super-popular 400 cc class and in the prcess created its own classic status.

Suitably modified CB400F roadsters once dominated World Championship Formula Three racing; Rob Claude, seen here at Ballacraine on the TT course during the late 1970s being one of the better known exponents

XL250, first 4-valve — and a bland best seller

At last the Stateside arm of Honda had responded to countless calls for the market leaders to offer a genuine green lanes four-stroke single. As 1972 dawned the company was finally in the position to come up with one of its all time great bikes, the all new XL250 (known in some markets as the SL250S).

At the conclusion of Honda's week-long 4000 member dealer convention, the press were at least given the low down, where at the giant Las Vegas Convention Centre, some 80 or so of the world's journalists were briefed on the '72 range, which as the American Motorcyclist magazine put it, 'the star of the show was the all-new lightweight four-valve XL250 single that Honda has created to take dead aim at the two-stroke off-road market'. ('Off-road', in reality meant what we now call trail riding!).

To fully appreciate the background to this important launch one must recall that in the previous thirteen years following their arrival on American shores, the directors of the American Honda Company had earned themselves quite a reputation. In typical fashion — as most will now recognise, these Japanese and their carefully selected American lieutenants were not only aggressive salesmen, but also innovative, dedicated and extremely sensitive to the mood of their new land. They had in fact, not only done a Pearl Harbour on the motorcycle industry, but by this time almost won the war too!

Skirting the tactics which brought them early fame in Europe, Honda had shied away from race competition in America, pursuing instead the more practical needs of the average rider, both on and off road. With the now famous 'You meet the nicest people on a Honda', the Japanese had promoted their motorcycles for all the family. This was in complete contrast to how the motorcycle had previously been portrayed. Stateside it had been promoted, first by the American's themselves, and later by the Europeans, as an enthusiast only vehicle — which of course had effectively blocked mass sales.

In those thirteen years since 1959, America Honda had carved out their clear number one position, which had effectively seen off first the Germans, then the Italians and finally the British. Honda had concentrated their efforts largely upon the touring market, epitomised by the ultra successful 350 Hawk and the 500 and 750 fours, with rare exceptions in endurance oriented events (like the Baja desert race), their off-road offerings furthered the happy but innocuous play-bike

As 1972 dawned Honda was at last able to offer its customers a production bike with the four-valve technology developed on its racing bikes; this was the all-new XL250 (known in some markets as the SL250S)

image. And so it continued through 1971.

Whether it was Honda's sensitivity to the four-stroke enthusiast's plea for something more serious, or whether it was in response to their own pride after seeing what rivals Suzuki and Yamaha could – and did – come up with is difficult to tell. But react they did and in late 1971 came the first rumours of an impending all new quarter litre machine which would hit the 'stroker' hard – This bike was to emerge the following spring as the XL250 Motorsport (sometimes wrongly called the Elsinore).

As the XL250 was Honda's first four valve production engine, it is worth relating its technical analysis in some detail. Taking it from the beginning, the XL250 Motorsport used four valves because this had been seen by the Honda Grand Prix team as the only way forward (except for desmodromics).

But unlike its two, four, five and six cylinder tarmac racing brothers, the new production bike used a single cylinder, single overhead cam engine, with chain drive to the cam. This was taken directly off an internal sprocket on the left side of the crankshaft and contained within a special tower cast in the cylinder barrel and head. This tower stood free of the cylinder through most of its length allowing ample air flow around the left side of the cylinder for equal cooling. The very short camshaft had only two lobes since each rocker was forked on the valve side to accommodate two valves rather than one. In the head, the top half of the camshaft was secured by the rocker box when in place, whilst the rocker arms fully contained in the rocker box above and adjusted by means of conventional threaded adjuster screws and lock nuts which were accessible through cover plates front and rear. The left (nearside) end of the cam carried the contact breaker ignition. The camshaft, by the way, ran direct in the aluminium — a feature which Honda had used on its smaller engines as well as their CB500 four. Combustion pressure sealing was assured with a six-bolt head pattern, the bolts wide spacing from the centre of the head hinted of a larger bore to come.

What were the advantages of the four port head? Many. Although a few more moving parts were involved — two valves and springs — their use triggered a landslide of advantages — as both manufacturers and tuners had known since the vintage days. Most beneficial was the greatly increased valve area permissible, above 20% more on the XL250. This extra breathing capacity meant that shorter cam timing or duration of time during which it was necessary to leave the valves open to obtain maximum filling of the cylinder, was possible.

Compare this short cam timing advantage to a conventional two-valve head for just a moment; if good higher engine revolution performance is expected from a two-valver, it becomes necessary to open the inlet valve early and close it late to achieve adequate cylinder filling at high rpm. This was alright for high speed but permitted leakage, even spitback, at the lower end of the rev scale

Above
Honda continued the four-valve single theme with XL500S in 1979

Right
Companion XL100S used only two valves

Opposite
An XR500R pauses for a breather after some hectic action

The Honda Britain sponsored Imps children's display team used XL185

needed in a dirt bike engine. Consequently the two-valve head tuner had to decide where he wanted his best power spread – at high or low revs – but not both! This was where the four-valve design offered its biggest advantage outside GP racing. Because of their superior area, the dual-inlet valves, for example could be lifted later and because of their individually lighter weight, not only was the top end improved, but the excellent sealing at low rpm provided superior bottom end characteristics. In addition, the valves in a four-valve head could be considerably smaller which meant extra torque. Smaller valves also meant less reciprocating weight per valve, permitting smaller springs and better spring control. Although valve lift, rate and time of opening are determined by flow meter, the multitude of advantages offered by the four-valve design gave Honda engineers a wide latitude of movement in several directions in achieving the ideal.

Another feature was the narrow angle between the inlet and exhaust valves in the XL250 engine. Putting them more vertical contributed to shorter and therefore reciprocating rocker weight, less possibility of the valves tangling on overlap, and less valve head restriction to air flow with the inlet valves in the open position.

Yet another advantage was central spark plug placement invited by the four valve layout. This encouraged even flame propagation; the flame spreading evenly and equally from the centre in all directions. Also, the layout lent itself to the pent-roof head configuration which left space for a squish area at the outer perimeters of the head, giving the flame room to spread out as it expanded into the small flat cavities between the outer extremities of the head and piston. This squish area was extremely difficult to achieve in a two-valve head without choking off the combustion area and limiting compression ratio. In the production XL250 Honda did really make much use of this latter point running only a nine point one to one compression ratio, even though it would have been possible to go as high as twelve to one.

On the XL, the port behind each of the four valves was individual, with a wall separating the two respective ports of the inlet and exhaust systems rather than opening out into a common plenum chamber arrangement immediately behind the valves. This thin wall extended from between each of the respective valves most of the distance to the outside of the head in the interests of optimum flow direction and velocity. In addition the inlet port was offset to the right (offside) of the centre, which positioned the carburettor outside the chassis framework, allowing a straight shot from air filter to carb mouth to assist breathing at higher rpm. Moving the carb towards the outside of the frame also aided adjustment and eliminated much of the usual interference between throttle cables, tank and top frame tube.

An XR500R being ridden along a Californian beach

There were, as on some early Honda fours, two throttle cables; one pulled the throttle open while the other pulled it closed. The piston slide type carb was a 28mm Keihin. The 248 cc engine capacity was achieved by the relatively short stroke 74 × 57. 8mm bore and stroke measurements – identical to the Ducati single! Even so the motor produced excellent torque, a point I well remember from my own '73 model XL250 Motorsport. Sliding down the bore we'll now take a look at the bottom end. The crankshaft was pressed together and ran in roller bearings, with a combination flywheel and magneto on the left end, open side outwards to facilitate service or replacement through the removal of the outer engine cover. Both outer covers, (left and right), were in fact made of magnesium – a material normally only used on pure competition engines.

   The right side of the crank was splined to accept two straight cut gears and a centrifugal oil filter; the larger of the two gears serving as a primary drive to the clutch basket, while the smaller pinions sole purpose was to drive the tachometer. If the tacho was removed (for serious dirt use), this gear could be dispensed with – slipped off its shaft and removed to save further weight and friction. But its shaft must not be taken out since its hollow centre carries pressurised oil to the overhead cam system. The connecting rod bearings consisted of a plain bearing small-end and a caged roller big-end.

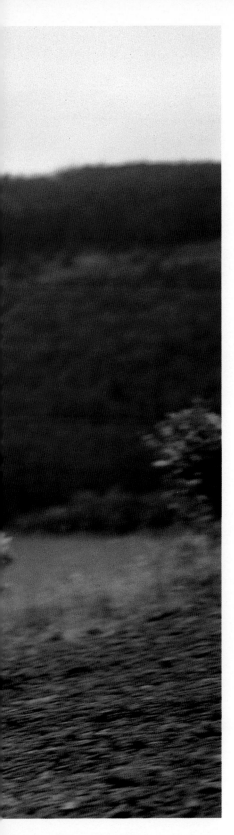

Split horizontally, the crankcases were very much in the traditional Japanese mould, with the bottom section serving as a wet sump for both the engine and gearbox. Oil pump was of the Trochoid type – which Honda claimed to be, 'extremely efficient, practically frictionless and utterly simple'. Well they would wouldn't they? Also known as the Eaton type, this design of pump featured an off-centre driven inner vane which rotated within a free outer ring having a matching inner profile. But since there was one less tooth on the vane than on the ring, the ring had to run faster than the vane in making one complete revolution, and the resulting opening and closing between the teeth meant that a positive amount of oil was enduced and discharged every revolution.

Oil from the pump was split, part directed to the gearbox shafts nearby, the rest routed out through the magnesium outer crankcase cover and then back to the crankcase proper via two aligning orifices at the crankshaft and aforementioned tacho drive shaft levels. One line, of course, went to the crank while the other was routed through an oversize cylinder stud tunnel to the overhead cam mechanism. Oil return, from overhead to sump, spilled over and down the cam chain passage. Interposed between the end of the crankshaft and the oil passage emanating from the magnesium outer cover was the centrifugal oil filter, which purified the oil before it sent it to the main bearings and crank journals. One other filter, a screen mesh, was located in the system, in the lower right side of the crankcase outer cover, which, like the main filter compartment, could be cleaned periodically.

The small gear which operated the Trochoid oil pump was the last gear in a four-gear train. This originated from another small gear on the rear of the clutch hub; the clutch gear which was mounted on the gearbox mainshaft, drove an idler off the end of the countershaft, which meshed with the kick-starter gear which, in turn, drove the oil pump gear. This design allowed the five-speed gearbox to be started in any gear simply by pulling in the clutch prior to kicking it through. Called primary kick-starting, this was to become an almost universal feature of later Japanese trail bikes.

The gearbox shafts ran in ball and needle bearings and were so close-coupled with the engine that one flywheel flange had to be notched to clear a gear. The sweet operating box was complicated by an efficient seven-plate, rubber damped clutch. If the engine had a weakness it was that the offside outer crankcase cover carried the

Dutchman Gerrit Wolsink giving his XR600 the gun in the 1983 ISDE

75

main oil passages to the crankshaft and cam gear, this case was far more vulnerable than usual. If it was damaged or cracked (which could easily be done with magnesium), the rider had to ascertain immediately, that he still had full pressure to the bottom end and cam. Otherwise the power unit was a real honey – and I, Mick Walker, should know as the one I owned covered many pleasurable miles before making way for something else.

It was also a very comfortable bike, both from a good riding position and because of its smooth torque motor and excellent transmission. My only real complaint was with its on-road handling which never inspired much confidence. Off-road, at least for the green lane work I managed, it was quite adequate, as were the small conical drum brakes.

There were quickly detachable wiring plugs front and rear to allow the lights to be removed quickly, but even so this was a trail bike, rather than a real fire breathing dirt racing iron. The mudguards (at least the front) were in plastic as was the chainguard. Alloy rims, without water retaining wells, helped to reduce weight, even so the Motosport couldn't be called light. The '1½' seat hinged sideways to give instant access to the battery, tools and electrics.

Besides the four-valve head and primary kick-start the XL also acted as a pioneer – as regards Japanese motorcycles – in two other important areas; torque and the use of four-stroke single cylinder engine for a quarter litre on-off road bike. First torque, this was the keystone of the original XL250. The Honda engine gushed over with superb low-end pulling power; it would pull itself out of almost any situation – and it made off-road riding so much more fun than constantly having to hit the gear pedal as one had to with a two-stroke of similar vintage. And this same torque hung in there too, right up to the 8000 rpm red line, pulling strongly all the way through fifth gear.

The other facet of the XL250 was that its success was responsible for not only Honda, but Suzuki, Yamaha and Kawasaki all eventually taking the thumper route when it came to designing a new generation of trail bikes – often of larger capacity. Motorcyclist , back in 1972 came up with a very accurate prediction. 'But possibly more important than the model itself is the promise it offers; I got the distinct impression that if this first bona fide (read Japanese!) off-road four-stroke hits the mark and achieves rewarding acceptance, Honda will be encouraged to follow it with similar four-stroke singles of increased displacement and exotica verging on 500 cc'. How right they were!

Even with all the mass of large capacity four-stroke trail bikes around today I personally still have a soft spot for what was a real live Japanese Classic, the 1972–74 XL250 Motorsport. Any reader who

Left
Another 1983 ISDE shot, this time of American Drew Smith creating his own version of the watersplash

Below left
British enduro star Derek Edmondson taking flying lessons with an XR350R

wants a good home for one in sound, original trim please write to me via the publishers...Over the succeeding years the original concept was eventually watered down, civilised if you will, but along the way it was not only used as the basis for the excellent RS250 roadster, but also even the TL250 trials bike; before being enlarged into such excellent machines as the XR350 enduro, XL500/600 trailsters and even the much-loved NX650 Dominator on/off road bike.

Changing the subject to something more important (in terms of Honda's fortunes) and somehow a lot less important: when Honda announced their line-up for 1974 it was obvious they were trying to snatch an even greater share of the market for small to medium sized bikes. Several new models, new styling, more gears, disc brakes and a lot of advertising said so. Were they successful? Here in Britain we thought they were at the time. But the machine spearheading this thrust, the all new CB360 had a hard act to follow, namely the CB350.

The CB360 was launched at the Paris show in late 1973; by early1974 nearly one fifth of all the motorcycles in the world were Honda CB350 twins, literally millions of them. The company therefore conceived the 360 to sell in at least those numbers if not more. Because of this it had an impossible task even before it went on the drawing board. The American magazine Motorcycle World went as far as to say 'If you're really enthused about 350 sized Hondas, then rush out and buy a 1973 CB350 because the 360 just isn't as good a machine'.

In attempting to make a motorcycle for everyone in a single package, Honda's engineers managed to fall between two stools. By adding a sixth speed, a disc brake (some 360's had drum brakes but not in Britain) and totally new styling they were also successful in creating a highly civilised but totally soulless motorcycle. Motor Cycle commented '...when legislators have finally hounded the motorcyclist to the brink of extinction he will probably be riding something like the Honda CB360 twin. It is a bureaucrats dream, quiet and unobtrusive as a Swiss watch, reliable as Big Ben, clean and tidy enough to be parked in the lobby of the Dorchester, comfortable as an easy chair and a willing starter. It never begs to be ridden fast. That's just as well as the handling on the open road left plenty to be desired. As a result the CB360 is about as characterless as a real motorcycle can get. True, it performs all the tasks the everyday motorcyclist will demand of it, but there's a somewhat bitter after taste at the end of each ride.'

Meanwhile another American Journal, Cycle Illustrated described the CB360 thus: 'Ladies and Gentlemen, The Rolling Stone. Honda's motorcycle for the common man is mediocrity with a dash of class'.

This final statement really highlights just why the CB360 has to be adjudged a success in terms of sales — in much the same way as the later CX500. Like the 360, the CX wasn't particularly fast, certainly didn't handle, but sold like hot cakes. To illustrate this, in its first production year Honda made 2,132,902 of them. Some of these were smaller quarter litre versions, the CB250G.

These were simply sleeved down 360s (67 to 56mm) with slightly higher compression pistons, 9.5 instead of 9.3 to 1. The smaller engined machine was only offered with a disc front brake hence the G only suffix being applied.

Actual engine capacities were 356.8 cc for the 360 and 249.3 cc for the smaller machine. This meant that whereas the 250 remained the same as its forerunner, the 360 was considerably larger than the 10 cc suggested by its designation because the 350 was only 325.6 cc. By 1974 all Honda twins featured 360 degree crankshafts and because of this they went through a vibration patch between 5 and 6000 rpm. It was nothing serious, just enough to be felt and get annoying after a while, particularly because this was about the lowest at which the motor was happy and therefore the ideal speed for gear changing and gentle cruising. Above and beyond the rough patch the motors smoothed out. Maximum power was 34 bhp at 9000 rpm, with maximum torque being produced in typical Honda fashion at a fairly high 7500 rpm.

Both the 360 and 250 made their British debuts at the Racing and Sporting Show of 1974. From a spectator's point of view there was nothing externally, except the colours of the side panel badges, to separate them. But from a riders viewpoint not only was the asking price different, but also the power output. The 250 version, in fact, felt somewhat gutless until the motor was screaming close to the red line. Sixth gear was very much an overdrive with the 250 capable of around 80 mph whether in top or fifth. To hold a high speed, the smaller unit needed frequent use of the gearbox using fifth and sometimes even fourth to hold station against headwinds or hills and for overtaking. By comparison the 360 had that much more torque and therefore urge, particularly in the mid range. For any given throttle position it would pull away that much better, and could hold a 70–80 mph cruising speed. Maximum speed was now 90 mph in spite of what Honda claimed in their press handouts. But like the 250 it suffered from being overgeared. The official factory excuse for this was to provide comfortable cruising without stretching the engine and to improve fuel consumption by keeping the revs down. Unfortunately this theory, in my opinion, only really works where there is a much larger engine and far more torque available than on the 360 twin.

Bland — but a best seller. That's just what Honda's CB360 was. In its first production year the company made a staggering 2,132,902 of them. Actual engine capacity was 356.8 cc (67 × 50.6mm) from the single overhead cam twin cylinder engine. Maximum speed was 90 mph, whilst a six-speed gearbox was standard

In reality of course even Honda would probably admit that the new middle weight was not meant to be a performance machine. Instead its attraction lay not in its power output or maximum speed but in being quiet, smooth and easy to live with. An unseen advantage of its relatively mild performance was that consumables like chains, brakes and tyres lasted longer, even the oil level stayed constant. All the rider had to do was add petrol get on and ride.

The large dual seat and soft suspension gave a luxurious ride but roadholding could only be described as the poor side of average. The machine had a rather negative, sloppy feel which didn't inspire any attempts at hard cornering and the performance of the rear suspension was good enough reason for a sales boom in after market units during the mid to late '70s. Again poor handling was a trait of the CX500.

Fuel consumption when ridden hard averaged out around 50 mpg, and as Motorcycle Mechanics stated 'It was easy to improve these figures by about 10 mpg but it would be so much nicer to be able to quote 80 or 90 mpg like all the B31, ES2 and Viper owners who are about to write in? To many observers the twin 30mm constant velocity Keihin were too large and too complicated with Mechanics saying, 'on friendly little machines like these I'd rather see something simple with a maximum of two adjustments.'

Almost without exception all the testers of the day concluded that the outstanding feature of the design was its front brake. Although it might have lacked the all out stopping power of a racing unit, the single 260mm hydraulic disc was much more progressive and predictable. Another well received feature was the efficient 12 volt electrics and the push button starter, a kickstart was retained as a back up. 12 volt also meant a 50 Watt headlight unit which was at least adequate for the machine's performance. This was in stark contrast to many other bikes of the early '70s which still retained 6 volt systems which produced a yellow glow from the headlight.

However, other details such as the upswept, rot prone silencers and the small 11 litre tank were not appreciated. Another problem was the side stand. On the earlier 350 twins Honda had had a lot of problems, mainly from American riders who'd left their bikes ticking over on the side stand for some time and had managed to seize the offside camshaft bearing due to lack of lubrication. The oil would drain to the nearside whilst the other would be starved. To alleviate this, Honda, on the 360 used a completely different stand. They made it longer so that the bike stood more upright, this caused problems for owners as even a slight gust of wind could knock the bike off its side stand.

So after all this how does one sum up the CB360? By direct comparison with other models it doesn't measure up. Performance is lacking, vibration is there and its road holding is far from perfect. However it still managed to outsell almost everything on the market, why? The answer lay in its easy to live with nature, its reliability and the fact that it had Honda on the tank. Therefore the mid-seventies CB360 is probably the ultimate UJM (Universal Japanese Motorcycle) and that alone rates it for inclusion as one of the most important motorcycles of its era – a classic of its kind.

Gold Wing

Following the extremely popular CB750 the Honda Gold Wing made its debut at the Cologne Motorcycle Show in Germany during October 1974. The period prior to the launch was rife with rumours concerning the bike's features, which included a flat four 1000 cc engine with shaft drive and water cooling, yet nobody in the motorcycling world seemed prepared for the reality. The Gold Wing was, quite naturally, compared with the other two long distance tourers available at the time, namely Harley-Davidson and BMW, although neither of these manufacturers produced a bike which combined all of the aforementioned features. The proportions of the bike were large, to say the least, and since its conception it has evolved in stages, the latest model being the Aspencade; powered by a 1500 six cylinder engine it is at the top of the range.

That first bike, back in 1975, was probably the origin of the term 'two wheeled car', many people saw this as a term of derision and consequently bought other bikes, however some 300,000 riders (260,000 of them in the USA) regarded it as a compliment and bought the Gold Wing. The Wing is renowned for its dummy petrol tank which houses the electrics, tool tray and fuel filler cap, the fuel supply being carried under the seat so lowering the centre of gravity.

The prototype Gold Wing was a flat six, single overhead cam 1470 cc monster. It weighed in at a comparatively light 220 kg (484 lbs) and had a bore of 72mm and a stroke of 60mm. The compression ratio was 8.0 to 1, it breathed through a downdraught two barrel carburettor and developed a modest 80 bhp at 6700 rpm. The prototype had a wheel base of 1480mm, a 20 litre fuel tank and wore a 4000 ×18 rear tyre and a 3.25 ×19 up front. It was capable of a 12 second standing quarter mile and a terminal speed of 130 mph.

The original bike had much in common with existing designs, for example the cradle frame and engine mountings were similar to the CB750 and with shaft drive the bike bore a striking resemblance to a BMW. However, there was only one prototype built and test riders enthused over its smoothness throughout the rev range, its an abundance of power and its stability, the only complaint being the poor riding position, which was due to the sheer length of the flat six, and so the bike was consigned to obscurity.

When Toshio Nozue took over from Soichiro Irmajim as project leader, Honda had already decided that a flat four would be the most practical layout. Hence Mr Nozue's concept of a grand tourer prototype was a flat four, water cooled, belt driven dohc, 999 cc bike

The vast majority of Gold Wings are sold in North America. The one shown here is typical of the many thousands which have been customised to their individual owners' requirements

with four carburettors, a power output of 80 bhp at 7500 rpm, five speed gearbox and a host of other good ideas assembled into one motorcycle for the first time. Honda believed that their machine was the first with water cooling but they were wrong; a Scott was the first. Nor was it the first to carry the fuel beneath its seat, however it was the first bike to use the AC generator as a contra-rotating flywheel to counteract the inherent torque reaction of the inline crankshaft.

After receiving favourable reports from the project test riders, who once again enthused over the bike's power and stability, and a further year's testing at Honda's Tochigi test facility the bike was released. It reached the showrooms in 1975 as the Honda GL1000 and so was born the Gold Wing.

Even as early as 1974, Honda were planning a fully equipped touring version of the Wing, almost an early Interstate, which combined Krauser panniers and a Windjammer fairing. Ironically the Windjammer fairing became very popular with Gold Wing owners, many of whom also replaced the stock shock absorbers with other makes, namely Koni or Girling in Europe and S&W in the USA. So one could say that these owner-modified machines were the humble beginnings of the Interstate (Gold Wing De Luxe in the UK) and Aspencade; Honda having chosen to uprate the engine, first to 1100 (1085 cc − 75 × 61.4mm) in 1981, followed by 1200 (1182 cc − 75.5 × 66mm) for the 1984 season.

Above
An 1100 Gold Wing out on test in 1981

Right
Honda Britain inspired gold Wing Executive with model Dinah May posing for the camera

Not satisfied with simply bumping up the engine capacity, Honda engineers then went for the ultimate solution – a 1500 six cylinder. Launched in the autumn of 1987, this 1520 cc (71 × 64mm) monster produces 100 bhp at 5200 rpm, has a maximum speed of 125 mph and weighs in at a muscle wrenching 362 kg (798 lbs).

Gold Wing production is carried out, not in Japan, but the USA and it is in this latter market that the vast majority of 'Wings' are sold; the machine being ideally suited to the American touring rider.

Gold Wing Aspencade in action on 'US Highway One' – namely Daytona Beach, Florida

Above
GL1500 made its bow in the autumn of 1987. This 1520 cc monster produces 100 bhp at 5200 rpm, has a maximum speed of 125 mph and weighs in at a muscle wrenching 362 kg (798 lbs)

Left
Aspencade details including computer screen facia, radio/cassette speakers, hi-and-wide 'bars, plus a mass of switches and lockable compartments

Off-road

Although Honda was the first of the big Japanese bike builders to go grand prix road racing, they were destined to be the last to enter the rough, tough arena of world championship motocross. Their initial test in the motocross GPs came in 1975, and then it was very much a toe-in-the-water affair, organised not by the racing department back in Japan, but by their American subsidiary.

Why the delay? The chief reason was purely commercial, Honda went GP road racing to establish their name on a worldwide basis and open up export markets. By 1967 when they quit, this had largely been achieved – they had no real need to get into GP motocross. Remember, that at that time Honda manufactured no competition off-road machinery or proper trail bikes which could benefit directly from participation in this sector of the sport. Remember also another reason: Honda's long time commitment to 'four-stroke only motorcycles'. Ever since the very early days when Soichiro Honda had transferred from two-stroke to four-stroke the company's motto had been Honda will never build a two-stroke!

By the early 1970s it had become clear to even the most die-hard four-stroke supporter that only a 'stroker would do in motocross, witnessed by the success garnered by the likes of CZ and perhaps more importantly Suzuki in this field.

Honda can largely thank one man, Soichiro Miyakoshi, for their entry, albeit late, onto the world motocross stage. During the late 1960s, Miyakoshi, then a staff research engineer, had looked around at the off-road scene and decided himself that two-strokes were the way to go. With typical Oriental thoroughness Miyakoshi taught himself everything there was to know about two-stroke technology. He soon had the rival factory's products stripped for closed examination in his workshop...

Miyakoshi saw two crucial factors which had been responsible for both Honda's success in road racing and Suzuki's motocross victories – excellent power to weight ratio. By the winter of 1971 Honda, through Miyakoshi's efforts, had a featherlight – high power prototype dirt racer – codenamed 335C. This machine featured radical port timing and oversquare 70 × 64mm bore and stroke dimensions. It was raced – without any clue to its identity – in several rounds of the Japanese Motocross Championship series in the latter months of 1971, but without distinguishing itself. However, by the time the newcomer was officially announced to an expectant public in the spring of 1972, most of the teething troubles had been ironed out.

Early air-cooled CR250 motocrosser, with 'Red Rocket' engine and twin shock rear suspension

The design, by now recoded RC250M, was raced by works riders Hirokazu Heno and Taichi Yoshimura to sixth and seventh respectively at its first meeting at Yatabe. In June 1972 a 125 cc version – the RC125M – was launched, with which Yoshimura finished fourth first time out at the Aomuri circuit.

The factory had gone for low weight regardless of expense and the 125 which Yoshimura raced at Aomori weighed in at an incredibly low figure of 70 kg (154 lbs) dry – 10 kg below the newly introduced minimum brought in by the FIM to rule out just such expensive one-off works specials. With their attention now on ultimately competing and winning at GP level Honda then constructed a brand new quarter litre motocrosser.

Known as the CR250 this made its debut in California during 1972 via the factory's American subsidiary.

Riders were signed, but although the bikes were tremendously fast they also proved extremely fragile on the ultra-quick, bone-hard Californian tracks. Frames bent after only a short period and stones soon pierced the alloy fuel tanks. If this was not enough wheels collapsed and swinging arms buckled. It soon became clear that in their desire for an ultra-lightweight design Honda had gone overboard.

The Japanese giant listened and learned. After every meeting a detailed report listing the defects and breakages was sent back to

Englishman Graham Noyce was Honda's first dirt bike racing world champion. He is seen here during his 1979 title year

Japan; eventually the bikes went back too. By the end of the year the machines were much improved and the production CR250s that went on sale in the States in the spring of 1973 were largely trouble-free.

Equipped with a five-speed box and producing 33 bhp the CR250 was soon followed by a 125 cc version; both were sold under the name Elsinore — after the American city where the cross-country Elsinore GP was staged each year.

For 1973 Honda signed the top Stateside dirt bike racer Gary Jones who had won the 1972 US National Championship series. Jones made it two in a row to give Honda their first taste of success in off-road events.

The year 1974 saw another Honda 'first'; this time youngster Marty Smith gaining a fourth place in the US round of the 125 cc FIM world championships.

The following year Honda entered the blue riband 500 cc class and signed former Dutch and American champion, Pierre Karsmakers from rivals Yamaha. During his time with Honda Karsmakers was provided with a succession of machinery that ranged from 360 to 440 cc engine sizes. Although dogged with injury that year, the Honda signing still managed to gain a total of 45 points, including a magnificent runner-up slot in the Canadian GP, to gain 10th place in the final championship table.

1975 had seen Smith win the 125 cc US GP, whilst the following year Karsmakers also made history when he won the first leg of the 500 cc Italian Grand Prix; both milestones in Honda's quest for honours at the very highest level in off-road racing.

More success came via men such as 'Bad' Brad Lakey and Warren Reid, but the real breakthrough came in September 1977 when Honda signed Englishman Graham Noyce. Encouraged by his father the young Noyce had started racing in schoolboy events when 9 years of age. Before joining Honda he had won the British 500 cc motocross championship series in both 1976 and again in 1977.

However 1978, his first full year as a Honda rider did not herald the success to come in later years. Instead it was the American Lakey who so very nearly became champion, only being beaten at the last gasp by the 'Flying Finn' Heikki Mikkola's Yamaha.

The year 1979 proved to be a turning point for Noyce... and Honda. The factory had also signed up the Belgian André Malherbe to replace Lakey who had quit to join Kawasaki.

The only real challenger to Noyce and Honda in 1979 came from the Dutch Suzuki veteran Gerrit Wolsink and even before the final round in Luxembourg Noyce had become the first British world motocross champion for 14 years. Noyce amassing a haul of 225 points, Wolsink

Above
*After winning the world
championship for Suzuki, Roger
De Coster rode for Honda in 1980
before retiring and becoming their
motocross team manager*

Left
*Roger De Coster and André Malherbe
lead the field in the 1980 500 cc
Swiss Grand Prix*

runner up with 177, with Malherbe, riding his debut year with Honda, in third spot with 176 points.

The history books then, show that Honda came onto the grand prix motocross stage as raw newcomers in 1975 and walked with the glittering prize in the shape of the 500 cc world title just four years later!

Throughout the 1980s more success and championships came, thanks to the efforts of Noyce, Malherbe and later a new British star, Dave Thorpe. The formidable trio assuring the name Honda was to become just a much a legend on the motocross circuits as the road racing boys had achieved in earlier years.

Finally despite the fact that Honda have never made such efforts in the trials world they have supported selected riders in both on-day events and enduros with a fair amount of success, not to mention the prestigious Paris-Dakar Rally and American flat track racing.

Left
André Malherbe, the Honda mounted 1980 500 cc motocross World Champion

Above
For 1983 Honda signed the brilliant young English rider Dave Thorpe to team with former World Champions Noyce and Malherbe; Thorpe is shown here during the British GP that year

Above
Besides motocross Honda also challenged for honours in one-day trials. One of their first efforts was this prototype 200 cc four-stroke, pictured in Spain during 1978

Right
Rob Shepherd competing in the annual Scottish Six Days' Trial on a works Honda in the late 1970s

Above
Stateside, Honda went flat track racing with machines like this XL600 engine device

Left
Another action shot from North of the border, World Champion Eddy Lejune in the 1984 Scottish Six Days' Trial

Vee twins

The idea of a Honda v-twin motorcycle is not a new concept; development of what was to eventually appear in the shape of the CX500 can be traced back as far as the early 1970s.

The first working prototype came in 1973 and was an air-cooled 90 degree 350 cc v-twin which was intended as a forerunner of a commuter bike of the 1980s. The plan envisaged a motorcycle which would be 'easy to ride, easy to start, had a comfortable cruising speed, light weight and handling with the woman rider in mind and maintenance free'. This almost perfect decree failed when the target performance of 80 mph was not reached and the project was dropped, at least in its original guise.

One important part of this prototype Honda vee to survive was the transmission system. This featured a torque convertor and a two-speed sub-transmission with high and low ranges; a modified version was developed for use on the CB750 and CB400 Hondamatics.

Another prototype v-twin, the A23 appeared in 1974 once again the engine capacity was 350 cc and it was air-cooled. Housed in a CB200 chassis both shaft and chain final drive versions were built.

Next in the evolution of what was eventually to be the CX500 was the A3S. Constructed in both normally aspirated and supercharged

After a succession of prototypes, Honda finally got around to producing its first v-twin, the CX500, in 1977. Both standard and Euro versions were built (one of the latter is shown). The CX was very much a middleweight tourer, but with an advanced specification

forms this was a watercooled, 80 degree v-twin with a capacity of 358 cc. Once again performance was sadly lacking (even in supercharged form!) and Honda's R&D staff reasoned that the only way of improving this was an increase in engine size; therefore the capacity was bumped up to 500 cc with a bore and stroke of 78×52mm. The watercooling and shaft-drive were retained but in some ways it had lost certain technical advancements such as a single rear suspension unit working off a triangulated, single-sided swinging arm, inboard rear disc and leading axle front suspension; plus of course the deletion of the supercharging system.

But at least the latter technical innovation proved of considerable help when it came to making decisions involving the turbocharging of the CX500.

As for the CX500 itself, this was launched in 1977. It was, Honda stated, 'a machine designed to be quiet, efficient, maintenance free (unfortunately early models were to suffer cam chain gremlins!) and pollution free. In effect it was intended as a taste of the new era motorcycle which, it was believed, other manufacturers would be building as pollution and noise controls became ever stricter as the end of the 20th centry appeared.

The CX500 was very much a middleweight tourer, but of an advanced specification with its watercooling, 4 valves per cylinder, 10,000 rpm redline, Comstar wheels, tubeless tyres and shaft final

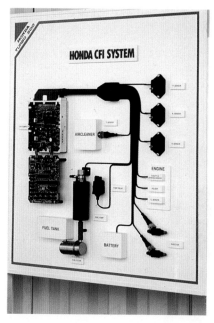

Left
The success of the CX500 led to a Turbo version which was launched in 1981. Although it created huge publicity, sales were to prove disappointing

Above
Electronic wizardry of the CX500 Turbo

Above left
Realizing that its CX500 Turbo was never going to sell in any quantity, Honda created a 650 version. Although it was a much better motorcycle this, too, never made it; but it did sire a touring version which was probably the best of all the CX lineage

Left
After the CX came the VT500E (E-Euro). This was lighter and endowed with vastly superior handling, but lacked the comfort of the earlier model

Above
In the important quarter-litre class Honda made one last attempt to create a four-stroke twin which could mix it with the best of the two-strokes. The result was the over-complex VT250; 35 bhp from the dohc 8-valve liquid cooled 90 degree v-twin still wasn't enough to match Yamaha's 250LC

Above

Honda's 1987 Paris-Dakar Rally winning v-twin was soon followed by a production version, known as the Africa Twin

Left

An early attempt by Honda to create a large capacity v-twin trail bike resulted in the XLV750R

drive. It retained the same bore and stroke dimensions as the original prototype and offered 50 bhp. Other technical details included a 5-speed gearbox, twin discs at the front and a single drum rear brake, together with a dry weight of 200 kg (441 lbs).

Besides the standard model there were also Eurosport and Custom versions, whilst in 1983 the capacity was increased to 673 cc to give the CX650. Both the CX500 and CX650s were produced in Turbo guise, the latter having a 100 bhp potential. Later models also featured Honda's Pro-Link monoshock rear suspension and triple disc brake system.

Back to 1981 and Honda introduced the brand new hi-tech VT250 in its home market. This featured a dohc 8-valve liquid cooled 90° v-twin engine of nearly 248 cc, producing 35 bhp at 11,500 rpm. Other technical features of this state-of-the-art quarter litre four-stroke included transistorised electronic ignition, 6-speed 'box, Pro-Link

Above
Transalp model on show minus its cosmetics, thus revealing engine assembly, chassis and exhaust

Right
In 1992 Honda finally got around to importing their VT600C Shadow into Britain. The styling, in particular the method of rear suspension, follows Harley-Davidson practice

single shock rear suspension, air-assisted front fork, bikini fairing, hydraulic clutch (first ever on a 250), compact planetary gearshift mechanism and 'O' ring final drive chain. Other features such as the enclosed disc front brake and its pair of cam chains rather spoiled the overall picture – as did the VT250s performance compared with the two-stroke Yamaha LC – and the Yamaha was cheaper to buy... The VT250 was to be Honda's last quarter litre four-stroke twin to attempt to match the all-conquering 'stroker twins as a credible sports roadster.

Next in the v-twin story came the VT500. This owed nothing to its smaller brother, save the VT title and its enclosed disc front stopper and Comstar wheels. The VT500 was powered by a technically interesting liquid cooled 50° v-twin engine producing 50 bhp. The

Above

*Testing newly produced NSR250
v-twins at the Hammamatsu plant.
The NSR250 has proved a best seller
on the Japanese home market in
recent years, often outselling rivals
such as Yamaha's TZR and Suzuki's
RGV*

Right

*The Honda v-twin has also played a
leading role in the custom bike boom,
notably in the USA. Lots of flashy
paintwork and bright chrome plate
adorn this 1991 USA-model Shadow*

engine fearured an off-set dual-pin crankshaft to reduce vibration. Other features included electric starting, 6–speeds, and 18–litre fuel tank and a dry weight of 178 kg.

The CX500/650, VT250 and VT500 were to be the forerunners of a comprehensive line of Honda v-twins including the Transalp, Africa Twin, Revere and Shadow custom bike to name just a few; not to mention the MTV and NSR sports two-fifty two-strokes which have proved best sellers on the Japanese market over the last few years.

Vee fours

Since their introduction in the early 1980s, Honda's series of V4 designs have provoked considerable attention, although they have never managed to take over from the long running across-the-frame layout.

For a start the first model, the shaft drive touring VF750S, was a total disaster. At first it sold quite well, but very soon horror stories began to circulate regarding the replacement, under warranty, of valve gear components. Was it soft cams or poor design? Perhaps it was a bit of both, but in any case this was not the model's only shortcoming. The styling was not appreciated by many, nor was the lack of any real out-on-the-road riding pleasure. All this hardly got the much-vaunted (and publicised!) new design concept off the mark in the way Honda had no doubt hoped.

Then came the VF400, VF500F2 and VF750F in 1983. These were followed shortly after by a larger version of the 750F, the VF1000F and the gear driven but expensive VF1000R with a full fairing. All the rest (except the 500F2 and a limited edition VF1000F called the Bol 'd Or) featured a small handlebar fairing and belly pan.

If Honda, the press, or the customer thought this flood of new models would solve the mechanical problems completely they were to be disappointed. To a lesser extent the cam trouble continued, but it must be said, only in the 750/1000 range.

Just as the whole v-four plan seemed to be falling around its ears, Honda introduced their secret weapon, the all-new VFR750. This replaced all of the previous v-four 750s. Technically it might have appeared similar, but in real terms it was a brand new motorcycle. Here, the Honda pressmen with their 'super sporting' definition got it right – as did the backroom engineering boffins.

In many observers' opinion (mine included) the VFR was instrumental in placing Honda ahead of the opposition in the hotly contested 750 Superbike category at the time of its launch.

You didn't need any paper specifications to realise just how good the VFR really was. Just a ride would confirm that this bike was its own PR man. Not only did it boast racer like performance, together with state-of-the-art handling and braking, but it also had the vital advantage of being civilised and well finished.

Proof of the VFR's rightness is that it has survived virtually unchanged into the 1990s (together with the more sporting RC30), whilst the remainder of Honda's v-four dream has been washed away in a vanguard of what might be called 'progress' by the market leader.

The first Honda v-four was the touring VF750S, but this was to prove a total disaster. Next, in 1983, came the VF750F (shown). Unfortunately, this too was plagued by camshaft and associated problems

Above left
Known as the Interceptor in the USA, Fred Merkel is seen here racing a VF750F at Daytona in 1984

Left
Following the series of problems encountered with the early 750 v-four roadsters, Honda built a pukka racing version with gear, instead of chain driven cams. From this was to come such successful bikes as the VFR750 and RC30

Above
The smallest v-four in the series was the VF400. Like the VF750F this made its bow in 1983. Notable features included enclosed disc brakes, Comstar wheels, 'Pro-link' single shock rear suspension and Bikini fairing/belly pan

Above left
Honda Britain ran a national race series for VF500F2. This was a success owing to the bike's suitability on the circuit

Left
The VFR750 appeared in 1985; like the VF500F2 this proved an excellent bike. Ron Haslam even raced this 'straight-from-the-crate' VFR to a top placing in the 1986 Transatlantic Match Races

Above
TT legend Joey Dunlop aviates his VFR750 during the Production Race, Isle of Man, June 1987

Above
*Next stage in the evolution of the Honda v-four concept came with the RC30
(750) and NC30 (400) super sport models. Roger Burnett is seen putting one of
the larger mounts through its paces in 1989 race track action*

Left
VFR engine exposes its technical details to the world

Above
The 1992 version of the ST1100 Pan European; a tourer in the truly grand
tradition and Honda's answer to BMW K100LT

Right
Cutaway of Pan European reveals liquid cooled 16-valve dohc 90 degree v-four
engine and its associated components; modern engineering at its very best

MAIN SHAFT DAMPE

Transverse multis galore

The across-the-frame (transverse) four cylinder four-stroke can rightly be labelled 'UJM' (Universal Japanese Motorcycle) and it is Honda more than any other bike builder that has exploited this particular engine configuration in a range of street bikes from 250 through to 1100 cc, ever since the first CB750 was launched back in the late 1960s.

The vastness of this range can best be imagined by the realisation that almost 100 individual models have been marketed: 250, 350, 400, 500, 550, 650, 700, 750, 900, 1000 and 1100 engine sizes having been utilised! These normally feature a chain driven single or double overhead camshaft, 5 or 6–speed gearbox, multi-plate manual or hydraulically operated clutch and two or four valves per cylinder.

To cash in on the 'Retro' craze Honda even recreated the CB750 (Nighthawk in USA) in 1991. This is a 'back-to-basics' street machine, epitomizing the almost timeless qualities that made Honda famous in the big-bike league. But like Kawasaki with their Zephyr 'Retro' four

Right
Based very much around the original CB750 concept, the sohc four-pipe CB550K3 as it appeared for the 1977 season; a tourer, not a sportster

Opposite
Multi-world champion Phil Read leaps Ballaugh Bridge during the 1978 Formula 1 TT on his works Honda

Above
*Britain's Chas Williams (1000 Honda) on his way to third overall in the 1978
Bol d'Or endurance race. Honda also took first and second positions*

Above right
*The 1979 Honda F1 racer with fairing removed, it was the powerful bike in its
class at the time*

Right
*The CB1100R was as 'hand-built' as any production Honda can be. Its forté
was racing or fast road use, the year 1981*

cylinder models, Honda have chosen to update the original theme with
dohc, 16-valves, 34mm carbs, 41mm front forks and although twin rear
shocks are retained they have an advanced internal damping system;
thanks to these innovations the 'new' CB750 features both improved
performance and handling over the original.

All this seems in stark contrast to the mid 1980s when Hondas
new range of v–fours seemed set to oust the long–running
across–the–frame layout. But just as other manufacturers have found

Left
Joey Dunlop racing a CB1100R at Mallory Park in the summer of 1981

Above
Overbored CB900 Honda seen at Daytona in 1982. Note air cooled clutch, special frame and massive fully floating front discs

cylinder models, Honda have chosen to update the original theme with dohc, 16-valves, 34mm carbs, 41mm front forks and although twin rear shocks are retained they have an advanced internal damping system; thanks to these innovations the 'new' CB750 features both improved performance *and* handling over the oripinal.

All this seems in stark contrast to the mid 1980s when Honda's new range of v-fours seemed set to oust the long-running across-the-frame layout. But just as other manufacturers have found out (BMW being a good example) the Japanese market leader has decided to stick with a proven and popular recipe – long may the UJM in the shape of the Honda transverse four continue.

Before closing this visual look at the giant Honda motorcycle company, one model more than perhaps all others demands attention. This is the fabulous CBX1000, the first production Honda to feature six cylinders. Its precise capacity was 1047cc (64.5×53.4mm) and it

Above left
Honda debuted the CBX550 sportster in 1983. Whilst it set new standards of performance, it was not without its faults

Left
One of the very first CBR1000Fs being put through its paces in Japan by a factory tester

Above
Honda's awe inspiring 6 cylinder CBX masterpiece

Above
Besides the CBR1000, Honda also brought out the smaller CBR600F. This latter bike soon built a reputation as the finest machine in its class with a string of race victories in the 600 cc Production category

Right
Honda's only six cylinder roadster, the awesome CBX, was launched in Japan during late 1977. It's all set to become a classic of the future

featured dohc, four valves per cylinder and seven main bearings. Running on a compression ratio of 9.3:1 it produced a whopping 105 bhp at 9000 rpm. *Motor Cycle Weekly* achieved 139.2 mph through the electronic eye during a road test shortly after the CBX was launched in Japan in late 1977. Maybe not a stunning performance compared to the latest crop of racer-replicas, but 15 years ago it could claim top spot with Laverda's man eating Jota muscle bike, as the world's quickest production roadster.

*Douglas Promenade, Isle of Man TT week 1992, and a VFR750 along with a
CBR1000F ready and waiting*